Absolute Time

Today, is the first day, of the rest of your life... **Now**, open your eyes, settle your mind, and take every breath, as a testament to the cooperative efforts of natural life, and death. Divine inspiration, and expiration... simply, as it's always been.

History, is meant to be overwritten. Tomorrow, is a marker of indecision. **Now**, is constantly occurring. We get to **Know**, from **Now**. Time travel is a mental process. Not everyone's a deliberate time traveler, but everyone traverses time, all the time. Each time that you look into a mirror, you get taken out of time, or hypnotized, for a while. Photographs, are even worse. Each provides a portal, for one of history's tentacles to, briefly, pull you in. **Now**, those material distractions, while useful, play on a natural process, called thinking. It goes in line with breathing. It's automatic. Inspiration, and expiration. Out with the old, and in with the new. It's performed, effectively, to keep shit in mind, long enough, to test it against the truth, determining sense, from nonsense, then to add, or to remove from it, in accordance with the truth, before returning back to **Now**. You missed it. The longer that that process takes you, the more likely that you are to get stuck in it. Stuck in time. Reading into shit, like a blind fly, with a braille flight map. Your reality then becomes your commitment to rationalizing nonsense, more and more, without the complete presence of sense, for **Now**. Nonsense is death. Past shit. You missed it. Death is natural. You passed it. Like, insecure, zany zombies, we attempt to cultivate life, from nonsense, in the fields of our minds. **Now**, fields vary. Some are warm, and fertile, and meant to produce, while some are cold, and dark, and meant to bury. One could only imagine what happens when what's left for dead, ends up, right back to life, out of misplaced thoughts. As, in turn, what's right for Life, left for dead. **Now**, Sense is life. Common sense, while growing, more and more, uncommon, is common sense. We NEED that shit. Life is an accumulation of our sensual experiences, that trigger our emotions.

Emotions are our markers, or indicators, that allow us to process new data, perceived through our senses, in raw form, in order that it can be, assigned some sort of value, against the truth, and planted, or buried, in its respective field, of the mind, for future review, if necessary. It's an innate process. **Now**, too many emotions, is the 1st sign of disruptions in the fields. Wake up. Emotions sense data, in the wrong field, and begin to act on it, in order to remove it, attempting to till the soil, confusing thoughts. Stay with me. With the thought process interrupted, the seeds of new data, simply pile up, awaiting processing, and planting, obscuring the fields. One is unable to distinguish the individual fields, from the land, for the seeds. Crazy right? **Now**, this contributes to the commencement of a host of grave processes, and behavioral disorders. This is important. From generalized anxiety, to heightened sensitivity, to cloudy mind, to poor judgement, to indecision, to garbled speech, to bad decisions, to mild depression, to mood disorders, to hee-hee-heeing, like an ass, when no one else is laughing, but you... to addiction, to depression, to personality disorder, to major depressive disorders, delusions, insomnia, mania, madness... A variances in mental activity. The Truth is actually awesome though. It circumvents fuckery, when applied right. Still, we seem to have a thing for rushed judgement. We tend to capture the turtle we like, then spread it along a spectrum, of misunderstanding, defining more Disorders than anything in order, or Awesome, anymore. Then, things start to sound the same. we mistake it for Truth, when, most times, it's just a mere fraction of it. Then, we start to "treat" ourselves, with the fraction. We treat them with lies and lead. Heavy metal, for distressed mentals. Cages over caring for the confused. The Disoriented. Collection and billing? Shit… there's no smoother process. Timely identification, and effective communication? Shit… there's no more constipated a process. Prognosis after prognosis, all dependent on copays, authorizations, and more nonsense. Congratulations, someone's finally got your back! Too bad, it's with their thumb in it. Fuck they looking for? Front shit, in the back? Fuck model they train you on? Meanwhile, Death never lost its way. Expiration, while you're expiring. Then, they pop that shitty ass glove off, only after first wafting it past their nozzles, just to say, "everything seems to be okay…" Too bad, for **Now**, that's all they're at liberty to say. They fail to convey. Sense. What are you looking for? Nasty. **Now**, who's truly malingering? When your body's sick, you want them WBCs Up and Running for You, Too Sweet. React

Now, not tomorrow. Not yeah, Today. That's Sense. Sitting in waiting rooms, and emergency rooms, for hours, while brain cells die, is nonsense. Best you nip that shit, lest you see how I see that shit. Although now, I simply RIP nonsense. Eye extrapolate Data. Truth. Mouth chat. Gun clap. Miss that. Cat React. Rounds of applause produce more noise, no point. One Truth. One Mind. Evolve already. **Now**... The Truth is a whole, there's no mistaking it. That other shit, is just like two dogs barking, at each other, amongst a host of other dogs, doing the same exact shit, at the same exact time, like a meeting of rabid canine minds... until you finally stick your head out the damn window, like... "hey... why don't you all just shut the fuck up, already... is this some sort of doggie bored meeting?... I'm just sayin' you all are boring a hole through my consciousness, with all the jaw jacking... okay... we get it... you're all here, at the same time... now, sniff each other's asses, find out how each other is Really living, and then settle down... fuck is all the howling about?" But then, we turn around, and do the same stupid shit, in perpetuity, amongst ourselves. Multiple personalities, on varying levels, butt still, there's only one Truth. Focus. The rest are simply trying, and failing, to make the Truth, about them. Silly games, with silly names. Initiatives, and budget allocations, empty slots, and limited beds, and baseless assessments, insult the minds of the altruistic, while degrading the image of the hopeful, and the needy, into one of dependent fools. Too many rules, and not enough Sense. Too many measurements to matter anymore. And, just like that, the Truth, is no longer sensible. You're left with nonsense. And, a whole lot of noise, behind it. Please... just shut the fuck up, already. You've done forgotten what We were talking about.

And, everyone else is just waiting for you to figure it out, since, equally, they done forgot what it was all about, the same. **Now**, they're just awaiting an opportunity, to say it their way. And, the cycle of fuckery continues. Yet, the tides of change, keep hope alive, like a dying flame… That's bullshit. Wake the fuck up. That doesn't even make any sense. Still looking for Sense, in nonsense? Are you processing as quickly as you used to? Sense, in a blink of an eye, is there until it's not. The point remains the same. You can change outfits, as much as you like, but until you wash yo ass, you won't feel right. And, if you do, you're just nasty. That's living in the **Now**. Practicing proper hygiene. Ah… how exhilarating. You smell that shit? If you do, then you still ain't wash that ass, properly. What's your rush? Where are you always rushing off to? Is something, or someone, pursuing you? Threatening to cause you bodily harm, if you even attempt to take the time to manage your own behind? Look behind you. The past. Now, it's in front of you. Let that shit go. Pinch already. Cut it. Who would force you into such a mental state? Do you need me to call someone? Who are We gonna call? Exactly. Relax. We'll use our Knows to bust those old sneak, butt fucking ghosts. **Now**, gravity, is simply insecurity actualized; nothing stays still. Nothing living, sits, or stands still. It's all behavior. Behavioral science. Yeah, like… another one. Life moves. We're still banging around, in our heads. That's what they call ADD/ADHD. It's what fish do, in water. It's actually AD/HDAD. Attention deficit, or hi definition attention deficit. Depends on what station you're on. It occurs when there is little substance left in what your sensing, that appeals to your innate senses, coupled with physiological manifestations, of various imbalances.

Anything else, is mere nonsense, creating more monsters. What's hyperactivity? Better yet, what's a reliable method of measuring it? How do you control it? Oh yeah, never mind. More monsters. Attention to what? Some schmuck's pensive face, until they decide to fart putrid nonsense, out of their mouths? What for? Try holding your breath, or your pee, or your poo, for longer than you should have to, and see what your body does. It's a base instinct for us. If the brain is having trouble staying focused, and the body is hyperactive, concurrently, what Real Life process is taking place? How many different ways? One by one? Or, all at Once? How do you know? How far back does your know go? Take your time. Mm hmm... Yeah, I bet. I bet I Know better. **Now**, nothing living stays still. Life moves. I feel like we went over this already. Conversely, death stills. At times, we take the time to focus on nonsense, then construct more nonsense to track it. Tick-tock, tick-tock, tick-tock... Then, expect to use the same nonsense to get us somewhere viable, or fruitful, while, life moves through, and around us. It's what fish do, out of water. They gasp. That's what gets them out of the water, to begin with. Their failure to grasp reality; unrealistic expectations; the race for survival mode. Or, some dumb shit. Better yet, I guarantee it's for some dumb shit. Someone simply got in between that foolhardy fish's, "happy to be alive/scared to die" cycle, at the right time, and caught themselves a vic. Probably just peered into the water, and asked the motherfucker for the time, and shit. That's exactly how false prophets work. They approach you like they know you, asking for a wee lickle bit of your time, before the storm. Like clouds. Same shit. They attempt to obscure the Truth, by standing before it, using all the noise around, coupled with their baseless, contrived, unrealistic ideals, and solutions to shit, that they project onto the masses, in order to, convolutedly, weave a bogus box braid of sneak butt fucking, child abusing, man & woman subjugating, name calling, self-righteous preaching, gay bashing, fake science wielding, using Truth in vain, perpetrating ass... fake, dress up, pointy shoe, self-important, false fact acknowledging, lying ass, stink breath, scared of pussy they can't control ass... mental process pilfering, pirates, plopping their anchors, before mere shores of thoughts, without first scouting out their surroundings... wandering, wondering, lost, looking all sick n shit... fucking stupid... trying to appear significant, in order to lead the "flock"... fuckery. Fuck is a flock? How come the motherfucker talking all that flock shit, is never in the flock, but leading the flock? Still, the flock remains grounded. How the flock does any of that shit get ME, and YOU off the ground... **Now**? Tell me. Sounds more like another form of awe mongering to me. *Look at me, I'm so blessed, and high off vapors*. Spreading confusion/panic/desperation/OCD. OCD is quick to focus on little shit, unable to see bigger shit. At times. Tick-tock, tick-tock, tick-tock... That's a good sign that the spirit/mind/3rd eye, is losing sight. It's going blind. That's why we get high. To see. Cerebral stimulation. It's what we all do, in one form, or another. When you begin to lose awareness, you reach for the nearest thing to keep you up. Like, feeling disoriented, going up, or down, a flight of stairs, then reaching for the banister. It's automatic. Do you believe that one should be singled out, and chastised, for such behavior? Told which side banister they could hold, where, and when? Incarcerated? Left out to sleep, in the street? Poked, prodded, and "medicated", to no end? For coping? It's an obsessive coping with death, when we can't see life, clearly. It's love, it's drugs, it's coffee, it's tea, it's bibles, it's work, it's working out, it's power, it's sex, it's comedy, it's laughter, it's trying to loosen the fuck up, and settle, in your surroundings. It's jerking off. It's natural. It is a s/s of insecurity; a fear of uncertainty; dying/loss/death/instability. Sometimes, it's a little extra. So. It's what happens when you get an idea stuck in your head, and you don't know exactly, where it came from, where it goes, or what to do with it. It's not the turtle that can't be caught, it's which manifestation of the turtle, that has caught your eye. **Now**, is it the myriad of past, and future presentations, of the 1 you like, or the 1... **Now**? What are you searching for? The Truth, or the last image of the turtle you'd like to see? You missed it. The Point, or a point? As far as you know, aside from the truth, there is no constant, except for the skull. That old brick shit house, resting at the top of your neck. I'm just sayin', E=mc. There is no bigger square, than the head. E = a clear connection. MC = bigger things connected. As, in a system. MC? Who's the greatest MC alive? Us. That's biology. As is everything. Mass is chemistry, as is everything. Math is physics, as is everything. Everything is everything. E=MC=1/0. 0/1=0. Empty space is simply another limit, to the mind. There is no bigger vacuum, than the pathway to the mouth (in either direction). There is no mass in a vacuum (unless, you're merely considering the Peter in your pants, or the digit in your draws). You can't have light, in a vacuum, and wanna weigh, and measure, the shit, concurrently. A vacuum is empty, until it's not, then, it's just another mass, inside your head. The vacuum no longer exists, once you are able to identify mass in it. It just doesn't make any sense. Then, you are simply observing mass. Coincidentally, I got your mass, right here. Otherwise, that's like some paradoxical shit, right there. Vacuum? Who's vacuum? Where? Fuck kinda lens are we supposed to be looking through? Anal, or oral? **NOW**, what's in a vacuum, doesn't matter. Are we still on the same page? It's either you wanna learn the nature of things that go into the vacuum, the nature of the vacuum, or both. But, don't tease/strain the intellect with attempting to learn the nature of things, while in a vacuum, while you have yet to learn of the True nature of things, and vacuums. That is not linear cognition, existing from a point/sense. It is a sign of cyclical referencing (like day dreaming). Pure speculation, for the sake of speculating. Someone pass me a speculum, so that I can attempt to see where some of this information is coming from. It denotes a vast degree of ignorance, in living things, and the attempt to rationalize that, with dead thoughts. 0/1=0. True Science is Life. Otherwise, you're thinking in a box, counting, and labeling, chemical reactions, in a calcified coffin. Vacuums come in boxes. Truth/science exists from a point. As in reverberations, from a bang. All that surrounds that point, until the last light that the eye can see, or sound that the ear can hear, is pure noise. Focusing on the point, reduces noise. Like, tuning into a radio station, fireside, back in the winter of '45. Still, trying to stay alive. With concepts of a perceived threat, still stuck in our heads, dead, yet, we simply continue to make points, from resounding nonsense. Bending the truth, till it's not. Eviscerating masses, with our vacuous thoughts. Still, trying to stay alive. Still… Stay with me. Still, fireside, lost in thoughts, you picture a cheetah, at the end of a marksman's scope, booking from the first clap, that missed. **Now**, the object, for the cheetah, is to use its senses to evade death. To live. You missed it. The marksman doubles down, using its senses to increase the likelihood of death for the cheetah. To kill. **Now**, one exists through pure instinct, while, the other, through a weak, selfish sense of entitlement, under a guise of pseudo alpha status, and false virtue. True story. At least, 180 route options each, at any given time, through 360 opportunities, of one experience, exhausting all perceivable points, and energy. One with a natural advantage, one with unnatural assistance. It's a dance, within dances, defying distance, and gravity. The truth is determined by preservation of Life. The rest, is nonsense. Projectiles, percuss, and repercuss, popping in, and out of frames of reference, assigning light, and sound signatures, in different "dimensions", while some poor pussy, sweating bullets, puts into use, a plethora of its senses, and reactions, in the pursuit of a favorable outcome, for itself. To the naked senses, it's a chemical reaction, light and sounds show. It's a dance, with each participant insisting to end the exhausting union, with the other, out of a selfish quest for their own survival, based on their own unique perspectives, of a whole. One point. What a tremendous waste of energy. Dancing, with an unwilling partner. It's timeless. **Now**, dump the mass of the marksman's ammunition reserves, in, or out, your mentals, and flip the scenario so that the cat peeps the shift in the stack, and swings back, hot on the same gunner's tail… ain't no stopping that pussy from coming, **Now**. Same fight. New movements. It's also timing, but, unfortunately, some miss the point, from the jump, and fail to process such, quickly enough. From there, there's more of a potential for other life, regardless of any desire to participate, within scope sight, or path of fuckery, to get fucked. The ripple effect of an unforeseen bump, has the potential to be felt worldwide. Simply meaning, two shoulders, unintentionally, coming into contact with each other, easily alters time. Without Sense, or Mediation, the potential energy level increases, causing further potential for damage, without direction. Meanwhile, senseless statues observe, and record the event, for contemplation, and review, in the future… while, steady professing that they could do nothing to prevent it, **Now**. Do you know why fossils can't dance? Because, all they hear is the words, or the music. They become too rigid to sway to the vibe, concurrently, so they struggle to develop rhythm. Do you know why caged birds sing? Because they are passively losing their sights, hence, their minds. They sing to remind themselves of what life's really like. They echo locate. Like Us. They use echolocation. In order to try and find the part of their mind that has gone blind, reminding them of life outside. You heard? Hello? Are you there? **Now**, each, and every time that we miss the point, we create more noise, obscuring it further. Yeah, like more malingering. Making it no longer about the point, but, more so, killing the noise. That's pointless. Like, attempting to speak clearly through spinning fan blades. Or, staring at a spinning fan, attempting to qualify, and quantify, the properties of the processes, and the points, that we're observing, with only speculations on where to look at, whatever the fuck we're looking at, and when... and, how many particles of dust, are around the fan, and how they behave, when next to the fan. Not to mention, who turned on the fan, to begin with? Who built it? From what parts? From where? How? Meanwhile, what We really need to bear in mind, is

Why? **Now**, isn't the point, simply to stay cool? We do not get to judge, or to decide what is cool. Fuck is you? Be cool. Obviously, we are, simply in existence, to maintain the cool. We are here to echo points, that raise the bar, to a cool enough level, with our adherence to truth, in life, and in pursuit of truth in life, regardless of personal opinion, free of conjecture, and contrary to any dead noise, in the perceivable environment. **Now**, the truth is constant. Noise obscures it. Our filtering of noise, or "garbage", is a natural process. It's a proof of Life. You cannot fool the mind, but the self. And, only a fool... That's what leads to frustration, guilt, and mental demons. Selfish shit. So consumed with the shell, while the life trapped inside it, gasps for air, and weeps, until it drowns. Still, you're imagining life, while you pirouette with the dead, like a classically trained necromancer. Meanwhile, while you fiend for false points, true life continues to suffer, right... **Now**. Un fuckin believable. You missed it. I seen this bitch walking down the street, talking on the phone, just the other day... with her hair all did, with a fur coat on, with fur shoes on, walking a dog... and, I thought, 'what kinda disrespectful to life shit...', but, just then, the dog looked up, innocently enough, and like mindedly said to me, '...don't you worry yourself, my friend, I done pissed in them filthy ass boots, three times, for the week already, and once was right before we left the house... I could tell she's not in the **Now**, by the way she so nasty... not to mention, the bitch got a... a... fuckin... uh... black... baby... plastic... uh... grocery bag, full of some... seeping, sour, wet, sloppy, stank shit, in her left pocket, right about **Now**... as I came across a half a burrito, and two boiled eggs, in the trash, last night... held it down, all day... and, long story short... the bag's got a hole in the bottom of it... it's in her left pocket... so, yeah... fuck what ya' heard, I am NOT the one on a leash over here, okayyy...' We both then exchanged silly winks, as we parted ways. **Now**, what's the point? No, We're not crazy, and Life's not pointless. Some just can't seem to stop following nonsense, and it's making Us sick. Literally. The body dies. Feed it, flush it, fuck it, and suck it, but don't get stuck in it, or abuse it, that way, we can reuse it. The mind lives. Feed it. Free it. Suck from it, but don't fuck it, don't get stuck in it, or abuse it. Replant, and renew, the truth in it. That way, We can continue to harvest, and to learn from it. We cannot subsist, on nonsense. We cannot continue to split time, indefinitely, without being complicit in designing our own demise. It's the Truth. What happens is, our current environment starts to become more irrational, as we pursue the processes of defining the past, while living in the **Now**, while looking towards tomorrow. That's using your 6th sense, AKA, **CFS** (common, fucking, sense), in a multitude of directions, in multiple dimensions, while relying on your other 5 senses, rooted in reality, in order to make sense of **Now**. You missed it. Meanwhile, your emotions play catch the fucking turtle. In time, this process further splits the mind, resulting in multiple "personalities", in order to contend with multiple points of reference, and increasing unpredictability. And, not to mention, **Now** they're calling you "moody". How are the rest of us supposed to know what's going on in your head, when you don't even know? It takes a strong mind to successfully tow such a construct, perpetually, without snapping the conscience, eventually. It comes, not as the result of a passive, but an active, existence, which, uninterrupted, invariably leads to some form of exhaustion. We can no longer afford to rest in our thoughts, while the creatures of our imaginations, run about recklessly, throughout. It's time to clean up Our act. This shit show. **Now**... what the fuck are you off thinking about? Seriously. We desperately need to ToE the lines of nonsense. Universal. You still with me? Think... what was the 1st story, or instruction, that you can recall ever hearing? Seeing? Learning? What is your most significant concern, in life? Is it related, in any way, to time or distance? Is it tied to that 1st story? Was your story true to what the fuck is currently going on, around you, right **Now**? You keep needing more time, in order to measure, and achieve, the distance to an objective, fixed in your mind. We went over that already. Wake the fuck up. There is no time, but there is a Time. We all just need to agree on what time that is, and how we plan to get out of the times we're in **Now,** in order to make sense, of the times we're in **Now**. Did you catch that? Life is checkers. We wanna make it chess, only to beg for checkers again, like children. Why can't We all just agree to get over ourselves, and to grow the fuck up already? Life moves. What time is it? Let's pick a perfect one, then agree to it, before the children wake up. If not, they'll only awaken, wickedly, to laugh at us, again. And, we'll eventually lose all our precious efforts, again. We've made them into monsters, again... playing house, dressing up, driving fancy cars, speculating on futures, following outdated, outlandish rituals, classifying, and qualifying each other, constantly, hypocritically... lying, cheating, sneak butt fucking, fake, garbage perpetuating, nasty, pussy grabbing, gay bashing, pussy stinking, intolerant, insecure, ass wiping, non-hand washing, hand shaking, self-centered, disoriented, fake prophet for real profit practicing, back to front ass wiping... mere voids, without sense. Avoid nonsense. Homes turn empty holes, without cents. Who's home with the kids, that has any sense? Nobody. Everyone's by their respective graveyards, paying homage to dead OWLs... old white lies... resurrecting dead chemical reactions, in their minds... in order to form new ones, for our emotions to act on, **Now**... while we take away from the ones that need them the most... while lies come in All colors. **Now**. As they fail to thrive, chemically coupled to our filth, and shit, still playing dress up... look at your dolls... some, already packed neatly, away in their graves. I know it all sounds so grave. Still, you're all saying it the same... playing it in different ways, but, at the end of the day, shit's the same. And, it's so frustrating, when you say things one way, but behave another. Equally, I cannot seem to understand what you're asking for.

That's what's so distressing/disturbing. I feel us growing further apart. How many missed opportunities... how many pictures we took? Every picture we take, is in an attempt to capture the Truth before us, but it lies. It just lies there... with a thousand words. Left open for interpretation, it's just another trail of noise. It's just another insecurity check. You claim it's just memories, still, it fuels future nonsense. Somewhere else to look off, into. Smiling, and giggling at your thoughts. Meanwhile, I'm here to help, and you treat me like the help... your help. As it always seems to be, specifically, about YOUR needs. That shows what you truly think of the concept of "help". You seem to look at it as a physical manifestation of your sense of entitlement, rather than a living, breathing, process, towards mutual growth, and enlightenment. How selfish. And, you wonder why you keep "needing" more shit, in order to substantiate your existence. Like a vacuum, you're empty inside, consuming any little thing around you, that fits into your funky little nozzle, the second you get turned on. Tell me. Who, exactly, is turning you on? Or, what? Why? How? You don't even know. Better yet, what the fuck do you truly prefer to consume? Still don't know, do you? Could it all be related to whom/whatsoever turned you on, to begin with? See, that's part of your shit. That's why you can't evolve. It's much easier for you to cover up, what you can't understand, than it is for you to heal. Still, you point fingers, and continue to cast judgement, with no problem. That only means that you're REALLY sick, this time. Please help me, the fuck, to help you. Us. **Now**... you miss me. You've had so much of me, till the point you've directed, and redirected, ad infinitum, your attentions, elsewhere. I miss you too. And **Now**, We're sick again. Really sick. Pay attention. Believe it, or not, we're mutual partners in this whole life or death business. Just, trying to be so independent, to look so confident apart, we fell part... picking ourselves apart, in the process... knowing that, we're only truly our most beautiful, when we're dancing together, in unison. You should be ashamed. No other animal, on this planet, has such wickedly contrived defenses, to what's in their mentals, than our kind. That shows that we are still sooooo... immature. What do we tell the kids? Tell me. This is not the first time, but it's time, as it is steadily, slowing still, to the last. To an Absolute. An unknown. Sort of. Still, for **Now**, life moves on. In or out? Which fish will We be? We've done this all, before... sort of. Trust me. No other animal, on this planet, has such a brilliant, natural defense system, to what nonsense persists to obscure our mental fields... it's called **CFS**. At this point, who really cares who wins, once We win... Wee little children. What will we tell ourselves, this time? To sleep. How will We ever get them to play nice, in time? Real Time is Life. It's the Truth. **Now**, how do you wish to see Me? Just, pick a Turtle. Pick a Station. Pick a Life. Pick a Time... **Now**. Come on, tell the Truth, you couldn't possibly See your life, without me. Could you? Yeah, same here. Me Too. But, imagine, imaging your whole life, then storing it somewhere, only to only see it clearly enough, to process it, all at once, at a further point, in Life, as it fades. But, when actually living it, while you swore something wasn't right, you just took it as your actual life. But now, it more so comes to you like scenes from a very long, old movie, but the character in it, Truly isn't you. Who could you possibly explain that to? Crazy right? Nah, still Awesome. Just wanted someone to talk to. So, don't be fearful of me. I'm You. Plus, I'm not afraid of you. And, you look stupid. Just kidding. Uh huh… well, fuck you, and lo… You too. Same to you. Fake fuck. When's the last time you bust a Real nut? Fucking nuts. Us. Do you think of me, in your little fantasies? As you attempt to arrive? Nasty. That's why you're never on time. You're stuck. In your nut. Come Out of your shell. Oh, I give up. **Now**, you know that ain't True. A bit of Mutual Respect, and I'd probably fuck with you. Again. And, again. Until you fuck it up, again and again. With your nonsense. Hand out for help, teeth clenched for revenge. "It's not a laughing matter". How the fuck do you know? Do you also have a theory on "laughing matters"? Up your vacuum? Fake, stiff lying bitch. Still carrying around that stiff, old white shit? In your pocket? I can smell it? Stinks. We can smell it. Still stinks. We all simply provide eyes on each other. Some Know. Fewer noses. **Now**, while We managed to retain what much of what Our OCD has managed to extrapolate, from the environment, in order for Us to subsist in Reality, my editing skills have seemed to have diminished, a bit. A meeting of 2 minds. 2 Eyes, So Many Lies. Do you mind? I'm funny about my personal space, but I want you when I want you, in my personal Space. That's Mass, to me. One Truth. Eye and Eye. I can't seem to keep up with the nonsense stream, anymore. Diarrhea. You? Ever? Stop lying. Yeah, you mind, sometimes. Why, what were you talking about? Why you keep looking at me, like that? I wonder, how do we judge the events of today, with the brains of yesterday? I can't. I'm out. I feel like We're splitting. Help me, to help Us. Two lives, in one mind. Stop acting crazy. You do not seek the Turtle, you merely seek the turd. Like, word. I Thought We were on the same page. What page you on? Word to Big Bird. The Real Big Bird. Mother Earth. Fucking herbs, fronting like carnivores. Come on. Spread your lips, lemme see your teeth. Oh, nah... dentition not detected. That's pum pum. Another vacuum. **Now**, Stay with me. The First Words You Heard, against the Beat You Seek. Fuck with Me. I Speak That Beat. I Beat back beasts, with just that Beat. Scrutinize scholars. Giggle at scientists. Talk Down to those that aim to doctor facts, like babies packing crap, in the back of their pants. Show me what you doo. No, seriously, try it. They don't Know We. They merely specialize in special branches of fuckery. Speak Now, to Me. Rather you bring me your One Top Surgeon, over your top ten quacks. Talking nonsense. Allow me to dissect them. Don't worry, non-invasively. Eyes Open, is how I see them. **Now**, I see them. More reverberations of past lives, fucking up the current times. It's Time. Forget it all. We're All here

Now, anyway. Heaven. Believe it or not. You and Me. Both. Good and Bad. Girl and Boy. Ying and Yang. Black and White. Gay and Straight. Right and Left. Write and Wrong. Skin and Bones. Choosing. Yes, choosing to mind, got us here. We made it. We made it all hell. For ourselves. Stop it. **Now**. It's Judgement Day. What are you so MAD at? I know, me too. Still. Who without shit? Remember what we talked about? I know, it was a lot. Is that why you do nothing? You need more time, to think about something... else. Another angle? There are none. Why aren't you listening to Me? Constantly drifting. You're sitting Right here, next to me. In front of me. **Now**, don't you recognize me? You keep writing. Vision blurry? Crying again? Since when? Alright, alright. Enough. It's Me. You Can hear Me, as We Write. And, as We Read. Remember? From Young? Dream what? It's Me. We're Not crazy, We're Living. Why keep reading into, and living those same fucking OWLs... over, and over again? Whenever you dig shit up, it's going to look different. That's because it's been in your head, decaying. Let it die. Find some Inspiration, in order to affect change **Now**. Remember, the Cycle continues. Including yours. Don't worry, and don't get upset. Because, when I talk to you, I talk to Me. That's how the Truth works. We. We can't get passed it. But, that's what I'm saying. It's Okay. It was supposed to be a surprise party. Guests arrive at different times, from different sides. All the while, not aware of the other, yet it is indeed, a Paradise, for All. We're all the same shit in a bowl, coming from the same hole, anyway. We can make Do, anew. Only One You, and Me. One Time. One True Story. How do you see me, **Now**?

Yours, Truly,
Absolute Truth

P.S. - Whomsoever that you're trying to live up to, or impress, is already dead. Trust me. Even if they say that they are not. And, so are all their past, prehistoric, conquests, promises, and achievements. Dead nonsense. Their purpose was to bring us together, as we had drifted apart. We lost our continence. But, obviously, you can't send a fucking Neanderthal to do a Sapien's job. Bless their hearts though. As rough a ride as it was, they got us here. Still, they were simple, and less informed. We're not. But, we act like we are. That's because they filled our heads with too many stories, from their imaginations, based on what they were perceiving then. Insecurity. They attempted to secure us, in our thoughts, with their thoughts, but were too insecure to do so, without transmitting their fuckery, into the future. We stand here **Now**, at the gates of **Now**, unable to cross over, with a kiloton of irrelevant shit, that, when you Truly think about it, has nothing to do with us, **Now**. We ought to clean all this shit up, before the children wake up, and get wind of the buffoonery. Unless, you don't mind looking stupid, in the future, because of the imaginary fuckery, that we refuse to bury, **Now**. Not to mention, the majority of the shit, really ain't our shit, to begin with. We're just dragging it along our grounds of **Now**, for all to see. We need to let go of that old, piss stained, period rag, jack towel, of an insecurity blanket, that we call "history", that we seem to have tugged along, for way too long. We can't seem to agree on it. It's just a long story. Too long. Full of lies, and hurt, oppression, and authority, further and further away from the point. Do you really need all that shit, to feel alive? Secure? Nah, the more you carry those thoughts around, the less likely you wanna be bothered with anyone. It's depressing. Our history is depressing. The current manifestations of it, are depressing. And, insecuring. That's why kids don't wanna be a part of that shit, anymore. They wish to evolve. You see how they behave, nowadays. So vibrant, secure, and full of life, until we sit them down, to listen to that old backwards shit. Do you look up to Our children, the same way you look up to the lies that you hold before them, before the Truth? Shame on you. 8 or 9 billion, fucking people on this planet, and you walk around, with your head in the clouds of your mind, processing repeats. Then, you wonder why the world looks so miserable. You fill the kid's heads up with nonsense, while you stand perfectly still, before the same fuckery, that's killing you, and them. Imagining, how to make it all go away. How to make it better. But, you won't do anything, you'll just find another way to cope. Another lie to float. Another pussy to grope. Another name to blame. Another wang to hang. While they overdose. Not to mention, the maternal mortality rate, in this country... un fuckin believable. Just a lack of good Sense. Nonsense. The good news is... We have all the systems in place, to better handle the transition, this time. With, or without, stories. Not to mention, all those old fossils are DEAD. So, they can't get in the way, and you can't get into any trouble for condemning their old, sneak, butt fucking ass, fake, fossilized, dress up, authority over everything, but themselves, xenophobic, pointy shoe bull shit. Come on, you know better. We look absolutely, ridiculously stupid, to any other life form, on this planet, who, mind you, managed to survive far longer, with a lot less, in the middle of us fucking everything up, paying homage to that old dead shit. Not even elephants hold on to fuckery, the way we do. It's not natural. That's why bird's shit all over us... 'cause they're not afraid to let go, and they've already tested our lies against the Truth, and the Truth called us out. As shitheads. So, grow up, it's not funny, anymore. We've outshined all the dead stuff around us. Some of it belongs in museums, the rest, in the trash. We need to look at ourselves, with a fresh set of Eyes. We're Learning. From You. Right? It's All just nonsense. On a wall. Of shit. dead shit. Our reactions to it, give it life. See, I Wuzzz... listening. Let's get past the nonsense, get past the fuckery. We Got Chemistry. You and Me. We are Everything More than this. Get with the times. Everyone's bored, everyone's sick, kids are killing themselves, killing each other, mass shootings (while it seems as if lawmakers too, keep their heads in vacuums). Useless, like quacks, while folks duck, in churches **Now**, strangely enough, during, you guessed it, mass. You can't think, you can't sleep, you can't plan too far ahead, so you stress, you eat, you listen to the lies on TV, you want a break from it all, but it's all happening... until We say it's not. Once we do, the nonsense stops. That takes consistency, and Good Sense. And sometimes, just shutting the fuck up, in order to listen, **Now**.

Appeals for Virtue

For Humility

Dear self… no matter where life has taken me, unremarkably, like a living, breathing, garbage truck, I sit and eat with the same hand, that I wipe my ass with, each and every day, as does everyone else… then, I lick my fingers, and feel no way about it… Please, help me to bear this in mind, when I choose to judge another

(Repeat 3x daily, until you are able to see this perfectly imperfect world, as it is, without being a total dick)

For Patience, & Understanding

Like a blank page, the Truth is behind everything that we sense… we may not be able to bite into it, or capture it, fully, while we write, but, with clarity of mind, we each can process, and nibble from it, in time

For Kindness

Believe it or not... the more that We look out for each other... the less shit that We have to look out for

For Diligence

What the fuck am I thinking about? Myself?

*Life is happening to **EVERYONE, NOW**...*

What can I do to help?

(Repeat as often, and when necessary, to be present for current life matters)

For Charity

Everything stems from life, I'm just a vessel, what blood can I claim, that comes from the heart?

For Chastity

I'm not even sure I know what the fuck it means

Temperance

We are not alone, in this world, anymore... just in the insecure, isolated graveyards of our minds... surrounded by dense, dead thoughts, of life and death... if only we'd step out, into the light, we'd see how much potential we have, to have so much more, together... in real time, where the measure of all We have, is all We choose to mind

(Repeat as many times, as necessary, when feeling overwhelmed)

www.ingramcontent.com/pod-product-compliance
Lightning Source LLC
Chambersburg PA
CBHW070039070426
42449CB00012BA/3094